*Better Days
Are Coming*

Better Days Are Coming

By
MON'ET

XULON PRESS

Xulon Press
2301 Lucien Way #415
Maitland, FL 32751
407.339.4217
www.xulonpress.com

Paperback ISBN-13: 978-1-6628-1705-2
eBook ISBN-13: 978-1-6628-1706-9

Table of Contents

The Journey of Two Paths | **1**

Jeremiah Said It Best | **5**

All I Want to Do Is Love You | **7**

It's a Three-Way Love Affair | **11**

Love Don't Live Here Anymore | **13**

The War Room | **17**

Another Woman's Grass | **21**

Vengeance Is Mine | **25**

You Don't Miss Your Water 'til
Your Well Runs Dry | **29**

A Message to the Other Woman | **31**

Readjusting the Lens | **35**

God's Favor Ain't Fair, to the Other Person | **39**

Love that Killed the Two-Headed Snake | **43**

I'm Movin' On | **47**

Proverbs 31: Virtuous Woman | **49**

We are Still Standing | **51**

Pray Until Something Happens | **53**

Foreword

There comes a time in our lives when our faith is put to its ultimate test. Things that come up against us will force us to question the validity of our own beliefs and even God's promise. Be it sickness, loss of a loved one, or a broken relationship, we must find the strength in our faith, take back our joy, and keep pressing on. We must encourage ourselves and know that better days are coming!

In this amazing memoir of triumph, I was blessed to share the experience of a woman who is a living testimony of God's favor, God's love, and God's power! The challenges that tried to block her only became stepping stones. This dynamic story is a great tool for those who have suffered or are suffering from the death of a marriage or even the closure of a serious relationship. Mon'et is very transparent in sharing details of the pain and anguish that she suffered in overcoming a divorce not once, but twice! As a God-fearing woman, she came out of them both victoriously! She is here to help others, both male and female, regain their power and strength in trusting that BETTER DAYS ARE COMING!

I encourage everyone who knows anyone who's going through the same mouth-dropping occurrences in this book, to get multiple copies. This would be a great gift, a tool of ministry, or just a token of awareness. So many others suffer through these same moments but are too ashamed or discouraged to tell others. This book could be a perfect conversation piece. This story is proof that no matter what we go through, better days are truly coming!

Dedication

I dedicate this book to my daughter, Jamari Mon'et. She has told me that someday she will marry, but she knows that marriage was not everything that I went through. After everything she learned from my journeys through marriage, I pray she remembers that marriage is sacred; it takes two; keep God first; keep others out; and never be considered the other woman. As a mother, you only want the best for your child(ren), especially your daughter(s). I know my mother was a very strong and wise woman. Although she is gone to glory, I dedicate this book to her as well because she instilled some good words of wisdom in me. She and Jamari have always been my inspirations. This book is also dedicated to every woman who has been positioned as "the other woman" when you were first, the wife. You can endure it. Reflect on what I did to make it through the storms. Life and marriage are all about what you make out of them. Do not ever stay in a physically abusive relationship. GET OUT; you do not deserve it.

A special thank you also to everyone who helped me along the way with encouraging words, texts, phone calls, emails, cards, and prayers. God can and God will guide you through life's unexpected turns; trust in Him and live life to the fullest. God gave me back double for my troubles, my peace, joy, and happiness. I give God all the praise and all the glory.

Introduction

A long-lasting relationship comes with a lot of hard work and dedication between two people. It takes 100% from both parties. Have you ever wondered what a long-lasting relationship included? There are a lot of things that can be involved, but there are some key and very important practices that must be used on a daily basis. Committing yourself to another person with the hopes of forever is not easy, but it can be done. Marriage is one that God ordained where two people come together to be like Christ. This book will highlight the struggles that can be involved in a marriage. However, there are outcomes from such obstacles that will cause the relationship to end, creating heartache and pain, disappointment, depression, sense of failure, and much more. This book will show how a marriage that was joined together with hopes of being together forever ended but still created a new path in ending. Being able to forgive and pray for someone who has hurt you on purpose can be a life changer. It happened to me, but life does not stop there; you have to keep it moving.

What God join together, no man should ever tear apart. My life's journey for marriage not only happened once but twice. I never dreamed of divorce, but I wanted to be married forever, until death did us part. Life did not quite go that direction, so drastic changes were made to be able to live a better, more joyous, and more peaceful life. Lies, cheating, physical and mental abuse, betrayal, and false accusations can create heartfelt pains that can live forever inside one's heart. Without the Creator being a part of your life, you cannot overcome these distractions in life if you do not do the work to make the necessary changes. Life for me, well, I thought it was a winning medal that I would live to tell my story to many. I always wanted to tell the story of how marriage can work if you put the work into it. I never thought I would be writing to tell the story how being married eleven years ended in divorce. Being the other woman, when you were to be the wife, can be a mind changer. Being able to forgive the other woman was hard, but by the grace of God and His tender mercies, I forgave them both. Then I faced the challenge of finding another significant other, which led to yet another divorce—yet I am still standing. I can only tell the story to help someone else make it through the unexpected challenges that their marriage may have brought or is bringing to them. Life can be unexpected. Yet, better days are definitely coming!

The Journey
of Two Paths

Today I have begun to sit down and write about my life's journey. My life has not always been peaches and cream. I had to deal with some dark moments. Despite the loneliness, abandonment, and mistreatment I endured, both physically and mentally, and living in dark places, my faith continued to grow and trust in God.

I always wanted to marry a man that was like my daddy. My daddy was a very hard worker and provider. I saw no wrong in him. I would be happy to see him turn into the yard from a long day's work. I believe every girl who has a good daddy like I had wants to marry that kind of man. It became disappointing as the years passed; I learned that Daddy was taking care of another family. I used to watch my mom sit under the shade tree on a Sunday evening with tears in her eyes, looking sad because my dad was visiting with the other family. I used to say that I never wanted to marry a man that was going to step out of the marriage. This created some toxic moments in my parents' marriage.

After being in different relationships, I finally met the man of my life in a grocery store. I dropped a can of Glory Greens on the floor and he picked it up for me. We exchanged phone numbers and we began to date. He proposed to me three months later, and a year after that we were married. I was so excited. I was a very happy woman. We vowed to each other that we would always be there for each other no matter what. We promised to love each other according to our vows, through sickness and in health, for better or worse, till death do us part. God said in His word, "What I joined together let no man separate" (Mark 10:9). My husband was a great supporter, hard worker, and provider. I felt life had so much that it wanted to give us, but we had to do our part.

Marriage isn't easy. I would be wrong if I told you that all you have to do is pray and things will get better. I remember sharing with him how it hurt my heart when I found out that my dad was cheating with another woman and caring for another family. At that time, he promised me that I never had anything to worry about. He said he would never leave me or take care of another woman and her family when he had his own. Well, that was certainly a lie. His actions, lies, cheating, and the divorce told it all.

Through our many ups and downs, we sought the necessary counseling to help our marriage. Marriage counseling is good. There's nothing wrong with allowing someone on the outside to hear what's going on to help figure things out in your relationship. I would advise anyone to make sure it is not a family member or someone you know. Rather, let it be a Christian-based counselor with some years of experience.

It's very important to remember the lessons you are taught and use them to your best abilities. However, to leave one's counseling sessions and continue the same behaviors is never healthy. We would have altercations in the sessions because he felt he was always right. He always pointed fingers at me. He never saw any of his own wrongdoings. My ex-husband had previous marriages that led to divorces and relationships, and he never found closure with them. It was extra baggage that he brought into the marriage. Although we were living in separate homes, visiting as often as we could, we spent three years attending continuous family counseling sessions. We still took family trips together. We continued to love each other as husband and wife. These times were very challenging and emotional, but we were trying our best to do what was right until distractions started to occur.

Jeremiah Said It Best

I recall leaving the first time in August of 2012. I entered into a Bible study class and the pastor said, "Open your Bibles to Jeremiah 29:11: 'For I know the plans I have for you,' declares the Lord, 'plans to prosper you and not to harm you, plans to give you hope and a future.'" That verse stayed in my heart and mind as I rehearsed it over and over again. I was trying to understand what God was saying to me. This verse has taught me some real-life lessons. No matter what ideas I had in mind to do, God would always change them. My thoughts and ways were not that of God's. When I felt like doing one thing, God would direct me in another direction. A great example came after relocating back to him; I did not want to allow anyone to cause me to leave my home again. The longer I tried to stay, the worse things would get. It was time to move out and move on. God blessed me to be able to move out into a peaceful apartment where I no longer had to allow someone to mistreat me and degrade my character. God knew how much I could bear, and He knew the exact timing everything was to take place (Ecclesiastes 3:1).

I remember visiting my mother while in the nursing home before she passed in August 2015. She asked, "Have you gone back home yet?"

I asked her, "Why you keep asking me that, Granny?" She looked at me and dropped her head as if there was something I needed to know, but she never told me.

After my mother's passing, it was very heartbreaking to the entire family because she was the backbone of the family. In November 2015, I was able to relocate back to our second home with my husband. After that Thanksgiving weekend, he started acting strange—little did I know, he was seeing another woman. The exact things he promised me he would never do, he was doing. He was caring for her, doing things for her children and grandchildren. This reminded me of what my daddy did to my mom. He would go to work, come home, shower, get dressed, spray on cologne, and leave for some hours to be with her.

All I Want to Do
Is Love You

After one year surviving breast cancer, I began to stress. My life was beginning to turn upside down. I was trying everything that I could to save my marriage. I knew I loved him with all my heart. I wanted to give the best fight and everything in me to show him that I truly loved him and was there to help him overcome his past hurts. He used to tell me that he wanted me to come back home, but he forgot to tell me that he was not being faithful. I reminded him of the story about my dad taking care of another family while being married to my mom. I reminded him how he promised me he would never hurt me like that. He continued to put blame on me and never himself. I continued to pray, asking God to please help us because I wanted my marriage to work. I loved my husband and I didn't want another one interfering into my marriage. According to Colossians 3:18-19, "Wives submit to your husbands as fitting in the Lord. Husbands, love your wives and do not be bitter toward them."

One of the biggest mistakes I made in my marriage was believing that talking to close family members of his family was a good idea. Little did I know, secrets will be held in secrecy. I would contact a certain family member about what was going on, and although I felt confident that this person was truly honest and cared, it was just a soap opera; they were being nosey. No matter what was going on, he could do no wrong. When a man has to lie, cheat, and put his hands on his wife, those are the worst things he could ever do. I was not provoking him; the evil and darkness inside of him was battling with him. When there are hidden agendas and darkness that someone holds onto in a relationship, it only makes matters worse. I would advise anyone not to put family in your marriage. Try to work it out between the two of you or seek outside counseling. Be sure to keep God first and He will direct you in the paths that He knows you need to go.

I asked my husband if we could have a final session of counseling to see where we stood with the marriage. If he didn't want to pursue the marriage, we would get a divorce. He never responded. He wanted his wife as cake and the side piece, his ice cream. But he did not realize that soon, the cake with all the ingredients to a good marriage—love, honor, faithfulness, truth, laughter—would all be gone. He didn't want to go the easy way out. He wanted to torture me. The torture reminded me of the story of the *Diary of a Mad Black Woman.* There were ugly sides of me coming out that I did not like. I would get very angry and we would lash out at each other. We would call each other ugly names, pushing and shoving each other until the police were called. His family members knew what was going on. I made sure that I was informing them. I wasn't sure what to do. I loved him enough to try to make it work. Yes, I was that much in love with my husband and all I wanted was for my marriage to work. I knew God was the only one who could help me through all of this.

It's a Three-Way Love Affair

After he spent time with the other woman, I would confront him when he returned. I would ask him why he wasn't answering his phone. He wouldn't respond. I would hear him holding many conversations with the other woman. He was spending money he could not afford to spend. The house was put into foreclosure because there were months where he would not pay the mortgage, trying to please her. Other expenses were nail and hair appointments, jewelry, clothes, gifts, fancy restaurants, trips, etc. He was always pointing fingers and blaming me for everything when in reality it was him all along. Be mindful of the ones who point the finger because when one finger points at you, the other four are pointing back at the accuser. Often times, the one who accuses is the one who is the cheater, the liar, the deceiver, the unfaithful one.

Whenever I confronted him about talking to the other woman on the phone while I was in the house, being very disrespectful, leaving me to go see her, he would go into an uncontrollable rage. He would start yelling, screaming, slamming doors, and telling me that I left him and if he was seeing someone else, it was his business. His eyes did not see any wrong. He was thinking with and using the wrong head. During our counseling sessions, these were some of the same signs that the counselors identified in him. These were typical signs of dysfunction, imbalance, bipolar disorder and other mental issues. Oftentimes, these were signs that steamed from a person's past. You have to look at a person's childhood and see what kind of life they lived; what type of family activities were going on; and what a person may have observed watching their parents(s) growing up. As the old saying goes, "the apple doesn't fall far from the tree."

Parents must always be mindful what they do and say before their children because they will mimic the same behaviors. It was so heartbreaking to hear him tell me things like "Leave, why are you here? Go back to Atlanta. You left me." He was trapped in a three-way love affair and it was in overload, a wife and a side piece. I learned that as a wife, one must never accept being the second woman. You are the first and the only woman. Marriage is two people, not three. The ring symbolizes a closure, and once placed on the finger it cannot be split to add another. Always stand your grounds and in your place because God sure does not like ugly. Trying to love two sho' ain't easy to do.

Love Don't Live
Here Anymore

I remember times when I would go to work and come home, he would have purchased new locks and changed them. I would call his mother to get her to ask him to open the door. I would ring the doorbell, calling him with no answer. I would call the police to ask them to force him to open the door. Once the door was opened, he would tell the police that he did not want me there and I needed to go back to Atlanta.

I would advise anyone to never enter into a relationship without having closure from a prior relationship or marriage. He wanted to torture me with all the failures, pain, and grief of his own life. At that moment, I learned that hurting people hurt other people. There was no way I was going to be truly happy again because he was the one who was hurting. Regardless of the number of counseling sessions we attended during our eleven years of marriage, it still did not work because he refused to get the necessary therapy needed for his healing.

While I was living in the home, I started noticing pool sticks in the windows, placed so that no one could get into the house. I would pray and ask God to help me to understand him, and if it got to a point that I couldn't bear it anymore, that God would allow me to leave without being physically hurt. No matter how much you love someone, it is not worth taking any physical abuse. If a relationship has to become domestic, involving laying of hands, it's time to depart. I may have walked through the fire and had a lot of evil bullets shot at me and hateful words aimed at me, but I made it. I was tortured in many ways, misunderstood, mistreated on purpose, persecuted, emotionally drained, and heartbroken, but I do not look anything like what I went through. God did it. I made it. I am still moving forward. A life lesson learned: Luke 6:35 tells us to love our enemies and do good to them. We have to start by laying down our own need to be right in order to win the argument every time. A calm word will kill the wrath of evil every time.

My husband would make false allegations on disturbance calls to police and then locked himself in the room. When the police arrived, he would admit he called and tell them I was disturbing him. He would go into a rage telling the police that he wanted me out of the house and not to ever come back. However, once they verified that it was my residence, too, he had no claim. This taught me more and more to be gentle with my words to him, and to remain peaceful, because better days were coming. "Take my yoke upon you, learn from me, for I am gentle and lowly in heart, and you will find rest for your souls" (Ephesians 4:2).

I remember a cold and snowy evening when I came home from work and he had changed the locks on the door a second time. He finally came home to let me in, but he was being so trifling and nasty. The next morning, he went to work but he turned off the water so I couldn't wash clothes and disconnected the TV and the fuse box to the heat. After waking up that morning, I noticed how cold the room had gotten. I tried calling him to see if he knew why the heat wasn't coming on and he said he turned it off. I got heavy covers off the bed and wrapped up just to stay warm. I reached out to family members, letting them know what was going on. I knew now that he wanted me out of that house, but again I was fooled.

I was told how to turn the water on to wash clothes and use the bathroom. I turned the water back off before he got home so he wouldn't know that I had used it.

I was so blindsided, being strong and in love with someone who did not love himself. I was heartbroken because I did not know what else to do. He was someone that I had grown to love from my heart in spite of his past life experiences and mental behaviors. I was trying to show him what true love was and how it felt to have someone faithful and true in his life.

The War Room

What is a War Room? This is a room where all kind of things happen, good, bad and evil. This room allows you to be free and open to layout everything that is challenging you in life. This can be on the job, marriage, etc. In my case, it was my marriage. The War Room allow you to write down requests of all kind and they are prayers that one want God to answer. It can be in a disclosed place where you feel comfortable to speak openly to God. There were times where I needed to seek God for myself and give God requests asking for His help for my marriage. After watching the movie, *The War Room*, I began setting up a war room in the back of the house. I put requests on the closet door, letting God know how I felt about what was going in the marriage. I know he would read them. I believe everyone need a prayer closet and War Room. I had plenty of information at this time about the other woman being in my house and my bedroom. I told God how my husband was treating me. I told God it was time to leave. I would go walking to keep a peace of mind. I attended church regularly. Often times, God would wake me up at early hours of the morning to go into the war room to sit and be quiet. He continued to remind me that I wasn't alone, and He wanted me to "Be still and know that I am God" (Psalm 46:10). God was working everything out for me.

Many times, tears would run down my face at two or three in the morning but I had to be quiet and just listen to God. Weeping may endure for a night, but joy comes in the morning, (Psalm 30:5). I thought God had left me. There was no way I should have been going through all that I was going through. The more I prayed the less I saw or felt God moving. What I did not understand was that this was the time when God was truly working. It was like the footprints in the sand—when you only see one set of footprints, that is when God was walking with you. My brother who loves me told me to just listen and do what God tells me to do because if anyone knows best, it is God.

Some family members already knew how he was; they were familiar with his behaviors and they totally understood what was going on. These exact behaviors stemmed from his past marriages and relationships. He always had a hidden agenda when it came to dealing with women. There was always another woman in secrecy, just like he did with me. When he called me, the other woman didn't know it and still doesn't. He pretended he was visiting certain family members, but that was not true. He felt we should be together but he still wanted the cake and ice cream.

I never knew what dysfunction was until the year 2016. Dysfunction is real. There are types of dysfunctions in your family, too. It is not a secret, so find it, fix it and break the curse to live.

Another Woman's Grass

While I was preparing to move out, I found out through neighbors that the other woman had been coming into my home for a while. She would come by even when I would go to work. I saw things in the home that he lied about that belonged to her, such as a treadmill in the garage and alcoholic beverages in the refrigerator. When I confronted him about it, he laughed and said, "So what? You left." Then I would hear him tell people he didn't know where I was when I was be sitting in the living room. She would call and he would leave regardless of how tired he was. He would spend hours with her. I never confronted her but once, which was the day of court. But there were many times I wanted to follow him to see what she looked like. I wanted to know what was it that made him treat me so badly. God told me not to worry because He would take care of my troubles. I remembered one evening he left to be with her and I got in the car to follow him, but the Holy Spirit spoke to me and said, "No, go back. It is not worth it." I turned around a block from the house and went home. All I could do was cry. It hurt so much to see how he was treating me, stressing me and talking about me as if I was his worst enemy.

There was no way another woman should have ever entered the home and violated my privacy, but she did not care. "Vengeance is Mine saith the Lord" (Romans 12:19). She was so busy trying to get into my yard (my house, my bed) that she cared nothing for her own husband. I helped to buy those things she was laying around on and having fun in. When God decides to pay you back for your wrongs, get ready, because God's wrath is no joke.

We have to be very mindful of wanting something that belongs to someone else. What looks green on the other side of the fence may not be as green when you cross over it. Tend to your own marriage and leave others alone. Knowing she had been in my home, in my bed, could have resulted in an unforeseen scenery. The Bible tells us not to desire what belongs to someone else. One of the Ten Commandments, in Exodus 20:17, says, "You shall not covet your neighbor's house; you shall not covet your neighbor's wife, nor his male servant, nor his female servant, nor his ox, nor his donkey, nor anything that is your neighbor's." In simple terms, don't look on the other side of the fence and think the grass is greener in somebody else's yard. You should tend to your own yard, grow your own grass, nurture it, water it, and do what you have to do so that it can be just the way you and your husband desire it to be. Any person entering into the home of another spouse or their marriage, you shall reap what you sow. You can't take a hooker and turn her into a housewife.

I think the hardest for me was finding out the other woman was still married for twenty-plus years to her husband, and that she had children and grandchildren. It was never in me to enter into a married woman's home and act as if it was my own. It was obvious that she wanted what I had. It looked like she wasn't pleased or satisfied with what she had at home. She was all about the money, partying, and materialistic things. Well, it didn't look like my husband was the only man, either; he was only one of the other foolish men. After conversing with her husband, I could tell he wanted his marriage, but she was too busy in mine. I had to learn at that moment that I was better than that. I was, then and now, a true woman of God.

When a woman is fed up, there is nothing you can do about it. Elroi means "God sees me." God saw my tears late at night streaming down my face. God saw me in the shower with water rolling down my face because I just could not understand, *why me?* Finally, I was prepared to leave and move into my apartment. It was bittersweet because I had so wanted my marriage to last forever, according to the promise we made to each other. I never wanted to leave but I could no longer bear the yelling, cursing, and fighting. While living in the apartment he would visit from time to time, but I did not have to put up with his foolishness. I was living in an apartment for only two months before moving back to my home in Atlanta. God had finally brought me home to my baby girl.

Vengeance Is Mine

I recall one day going to the mailbox after he had gone out of town and finding a bank statement in the mail. I wasn't going to open it, but the Holy Spirit spoke to me and said, "Open it," so I did. When I saw the evidence of him paying for hotel rooms, bank accounts being overdrawn numerous times, purchases at nail salons, and restaurants bills, with our house in foreclosure, I knew it was evidence that I could use for a divorce. So, I kept all those papers for evidence when I filed the divorce.

One day in particular, I remember a friend of mine was on the phone speaking in tongues. When a voice was heard speaking in tongues, my husband would go into the other room. When my conversation started again, my husband came back in with rage and anger. He ripped all the war room prayer requests off the door and stomped on them, cursing and yelling. As I was closing the door, he shoved the door on my hand, causing it to swell. The police had already warned us if they came back to that house that day somebody was going to jail. So, he hid out in the garage when the police arrived and they later took him to jail. I don't know what he told his mother to this day, but whatever it was he told her, he lied. She stopped speaking to me and it broke my heart. I had known her for twelve years, and I had nothing but great respect and love for her.

The following week, he took my clothes and threw them out of the master bedroom, down the hallway, and onto the floor. I was sleeping in the other room the last two months before I moved out in May 2016. He continued to force himself into my room after I locked the door at night. He would use a knife to open the door and would force himself on me to have sex. He would keep me up all night knowing I had to go to work. There were times the other woman wasn't around so he yelled, screamed, and made false accusations against me because he could not be with her. Well, what would you expect if it was another man's wife? I remember asking him, if the woman he was messing around with got cancer, would he leave her and treat her the way he treated me?

He responded with a smile: "Yes, I would!" I smiled back and I shook my head.

The tongue has the power of life and death, and those who love it will eat its fruit (Proverbs 18:21). The words we speak can either give a person life or cause them to be ruined. When you mistreat the one who loves you, the one you think loves you will only use you to get what they want. It is not about love or respect from the one you think cares, it is only what you can give them. As a reminder, material things ruin and fade, but LOVE will last forever when it is given from the heart.

I knew love then and I know love now. I reminded him that in our vows I made the promise to love him until death did us part, and he will always live in my heart. I am sure everyone has somebody that they truly love in their heart.

You Don't Miss Your Water 'til Your Well Runs Dry

Often times we make stupid decisions that can become permanent over a temporary situation. Do not make permanent decisions and regret the decisions later in life; this gets you nowhere. I encourage you, who are reading this book to be mindful of who or what you run after. It could make you lose the best thing that God could have ever given you. Ask yourself, is it really worth losing what you have for someone else's belongings?

I remember the song "You Don't Miss Your Water 'til Your Well Runs Dry." He got angry when he found out I had moved because he no longer had the cake and ice cream. After moving back to Atlanta, I was going through so much pain and hurt. All I wanted was for the man I was in love with and married to just to love me like I loved him. I would receive many calls from him crying. He said the walls were closing in on him. The house was meant for me and my daughter to be there with him and nobody else. He didn't feel it was supposed to be this way. There were times he wanted to visit me in Atlanta and I would not agree to it.

Be careful how you treat loved ones because you will reap what you sow. I reminded him that I came back and I took a lot of physical and mental abuse from him that I should not have taken. I reminded him that he chose another man's cheating wife over his own faithful and devoted wife. I was not trying to throw any 'shade' at him, I was just keeping it real and having no remorse about it. Reality had settled in on me, and I knew I could never go back to him—at least not in that house. There were too many unwarranted memories that should have never been in that house.

He would talk about the good times we shared, the family trips out of state to visit family, family reunions, the chillout times with family and friends. He would remind me of the things we said we would do when we grew older. There were many reminders that he continued to bring up knowing the life we had was real. God had a lot in store for us, but it takes two to make a marriage, not one. A man can never cheat and think his wife will forget it. However, the same goes for a man, too. Cheating only causes a lot of hurt, pain, tears, regrets. and disappointments, and somebody is going to have to pay for it in the end. When you know you've got a good thing, don't lose it over someone who doesn't care about what they got or what you might lose.

A Message to the Other Woman

To the other woman, you were never worth my time and energy. You were invited into my home by a man that was not your husband. Shame on you both. You left your husband at home along with your children. You see, my husband made you feel the house was yours stripping everything he gave me as a wife away and handing it to another man's wife. You were in my bed, which was the most sacred place for our marriage. My flesh said to hate you and seek to destroy you, but the Holy Spirit said "No." I was violated and you did not care. Remember, sister: what goes around comes around. You have to answer to God for what you have done (Galatians 6:9-10).

It is funny when a woman cheats with someone else husband, she feel she has everything. But the pruning did not come from the cheating woman, it would have come from the wife. You see, the finished product was created by me; I got him to where he was. You only got the end product. Had you gone with the processing stages of the marriage, you would have seen all the behaviors and mood swings, the attitudes, the wrath of the mouth, the insecurities, and much more. Often times, she saw and felt it. Everything you get is what I was getting too. A man will try to perfect things with the other woman to convince her that this is the way it always has been. Wrong answer! It is his way of reeling you into him so he can be praised and considered the best man alive.

One of the hardest things was for me to do was to find love in my heart to forgive you, to pray for you, in spite of what you did to me (Matthew 5:44). I am sure those friends and family members did not know the man you were having an affair with was married. His wife was going through sickness. Some women can be very cruel and have no care in the world who they hurt. Selfishness gets you no place in life but a ticket to live with the devil. I learned never to try to compare myself to another woman, because I am already so much better than she will ever be. I am me. The moment I took my hands off the situation, I saw God fighting my battles. Often times we feel we can fight back, but I learned to leave it in God's hands. When you know you have done all you can, just step aside and let God do it.

Evil can come into a person's heart that can easily destroy their representation with God. We have to be mindful of our works and what pleases God. As long as I did right, God was going to bless me right. God was pleased with me and often times He reminded me. "For the eyes of the Lord are over the righteous, and His ears are open unto their prayers, but the face of the Lord is against them that do evil" (1 Peter 3:12). Sometimes love takes everything in you. But I had to remember that God is love.

Readjusting the Lens

When a person enters into a relationship after having previous relational issues and divorce, they must get closure before reentering into a new relationship. I had previous relationships, but there was closure there. I had to find a place where God was present. Once I found His presence, I was able to regain the power. Presence and power go hand in hand because now I was able to get control of my emotions, refocus on my life, and begin picking up the pieces. Only God can restore to you all that was taken, lost, and stolen. Even through my most difficult times in the marriage, God's word continued to give me encouragement. He was restoring me and reminded me that He was with me. Do not worry about what you have lost, because God will give you double for your troubles (Job 42:10; Isaiah 61:7). God did it for me, and He will do it for you. It is always darkest before the dawn comes. Set standards for yourself, spouse, faith, fitness, finances, family, friends, and then your flourishings.

I continued to believe that better days were coming. I had to do a self-examination as I continued to fight this dark place in my life. It was not easy, but God! When I made the decision to cast all my cares and troubles on God, things began to lift up for me (1 Peter 5:7). When a photographer takes a photo, the lens has to be fit to make the picture perfect. They may even have to change the lens for the light and darkness exposures to get a good angle and look for the camera. After adjustments are made, the picture becomes perfect. Life is not perfect for anyone, but with God all things are possible. Where is your life today with your relationship? What adjustments of the lens do you need to make life better?

Identifying a toxic mate may not happen at the beginning of a relationship. Often times people will show only their good sides until they get married. Here are some ways that you can identify if you are in a toxic relationship:

- The other party is always pointing fingers at you and blaming you for everything;
- If they did not come up with the idea first, then they have no interest in it;
- They always want praise;
- They blame others for their wrongs and the reason they feel the way they do about situations and people;
- Abusive name calling;
- Physical and mental abuse when one feels they have to put their hands on the other;
- It's always their way or no way;

- It is important to listen to and prioritize their problem(s), but they do not want to listen to yours;
- They constantly repeat their past, especially when you are involved, yet never want to consider your past;
- They encourage others what to do to better their relationships, but do not use that same knowledge and encouragement for their own;
- They are quick to identify problems in another's relationship but never identify the reality of what is going on in your own.

God's Favor Ain't Fair, to the Other Person

After the readjusting of the lens, I was able to move forward with the divorce in April 2017. Honestly, it was a very emotional time for me. This was eleven years later, in the same month which we married. While the other woman was summoned to appear in court and take the stand, the Holy Spirit allowed me to sit back, smile at her, and listen to her answer the attorney's questions. Her testimony was lies that my husband told me. She continued to throw him under the bus with her responses. She did not care that the man she was involved with was married.

After everything was over in court, I was able to leave, and God favored me. I was awarded the house but refused it because of the disrespect, rudeness, and invasion of my privacy. We ended up going to court two other times and still God favored me. I was beyond excited about what God was doing for me and through me. With God, everything is possible, but with man it's impossible without God. God favored me once again. Be careful how you respond when people mistreat you, because it is better to give a warm response without wrath than to entertain the response with negativity and punishment.

I knew better days would come for me, but I wondered at what point and time. I had to learn patience with God because He had me covered with His angels watching over me day and night. I did not know when, where, or how God was going to do it. God favored me in so many ways. No matter how much you love someone, especially in a marriage, never let anyone take your crown. God gave me power and authority over my life, and I refused to let anyone take it from me.

A few months after getting the divorce there were phone calls made to me during which he asked me to meet him at a hotel. Well, of course I would go because my heart still loved him. It felt good knowing she thought she had him to herself, but he would call wanting to know of my whereabouts. He always had that hidden agenda. I realize that when I put things into perspective of who I was, things would only get better. While he pretended to come to visit a certain family member, he was coming to spend time with me, and I enjoyed it because he was still the love of my life.

I always believed that my mother knew what was going on in my marriage and that's why she continued to ask if I had gone back home yet. She wanted me to see what exactly was going on in my home. I believe my marriage was reminding her of her marriage to my dad. Momma survived it, and in her heart, she knew I would too. We were both strong women. Again, better days were still coming.

Love that Killed the
Two-Headed Snake

I never regretted a moment of what I had gone through with him. But still, to this day, he's very dear to me in my heart because he was my first husband. Any parent who encourages wrongdoing of their child is dysfunctional. I wondered how he got so much praise for what he was doing wrong. It was only to make things look as if they're the right things to do. I wondered if there were any underlying activities that occurred similarly in his parents' life. As the old saying goes, "birds of a feather flock together." This can mean any two individuals or more doing the same thing yet praising one another for what they're doing, whether it is right or wrong.

In the following year, 2018, I met my second husband. I was able to push forward and date again and it felt good. Little did I know that less than a year after being married, I would be divorcing again only to learn there were issues with him that he needed to fix, totally out of my control. Things happened so fast during that time in the second marriage that it felt like a freight train had hit me. I didn't know which direction it came. I was confused, embarrassed, ashamed, and lost. I hoped it was only a bad dream. Deep down inside, I knew better days had to come. Life is not always fair. When life does not turn out the way we think it should, it is time to kiss the negative things in your life goodbye and move on. Some people will walk away; others may become bitter and hold grudges, but you have to kiss all that bitterness goodbye. I found out that you just cannot accept the good things in life that God has for you by holding on to the things of old.

A month after he left, I was able to join a small women's group at the church called Celebrate Recovery. We were able to share our stories with each other, listen to testimonies, and cry together. These were hard and trying times for me. I was able to forgive myself, find out who I was, and regain my authority and power. I was able to love myself again.

In one assignment, I had to make amends with anyone who had disappointed me in my life or for whom I may have caused any heart breaks. We had to make a connection either through email, letter, phone call to them and make amends. One particular Sunday morning, the Holy Spirit wrestled with me to send the emails. I sent separate emails to them letting them know how I felt about our marriage, asking for forgiveness for everything that I did, and letting them know I had forgiven them. I asked them to forgive me.

It wasn't for me to worry if they would accept my apology; it was from my heart. I had to get it off me and close those chapters in my life, because I was healing.

I'm Movin' On

God has brought so much peace into my life. When you are able to find peace, be sure to hold on to it. It may cause you to release some friends and family from your life, but this is totally okay to do because having a peaceful mindset is the best thing God could have given me. I give glory to Jesus and the Holy Spirit. Often times, God would tell me, "Peace, be still," even in the midst of the storms. I had to be obedient because had I not been obedient, bad things would have occurred. It was time to move on. Isaiah 49:18-19 says, "Do not remember the former things or ponder the things of the past. Listen carefully, I am about to do a new thing, Now it will spring forth; Will you not be aware of it? I will even put a road in the wilderness, rivers in the desert." God has begun doing a new thing in me.

At times, I have been able to reconnect with both ex-husbands. Interesting as it may sound, we are able to laugh, talk, and enjoy each other. They are enjoyable moments that I will always cherish for the rest of my life. As of today, I can hold conversations without entertaining the past because my past is just what it is—"behind me." The Word of God tells us to forget about those things that are behind us and push forward to those things that lie ahead for us. Have I repented? I sure have, but he who is without sin, let him cast the first stone. Don't judge me because I am still living my life and resting in a peaceful place.

I try to be very humble, respectful, and obedient, remaining at peace within myself in order to move into the next destiny of my life. I learned that one of God's promises "He will never leave me nor forsake me" (Deut. 31:6). I will never want God to take His hands off of me. I pray this book will reach many hearts, uplift and encourage many lives, and restore relationships—especially marriages. There was so much encouragement, wisdom, and knowledge poured into me while going through the storms of my life. Now I am able to continue to push through even when it hurts. I wanted to give up, but I could not. I had to remain grateful. So, I say to the reader, no matter the situations, always pray without ceasing.

Proverbs 31: Virtuous Woman

Who is a virtuous woman? I am a virtuous woman. I am one who help in the home walking alongside the husbands with integrity, discipline and excellency. I was that woman who tried so hard to lift up the spouses to make life better while serving God and raising my daughter. I never pretended to be better than anyone else, but I tried to be as good as I could become as a wife, mother, and friend. Often times, my daughter reminds me that I'm a beautiful woman and she's grateful to be my daughter. One day I will find happiness again, and this time it will last forever. I know I have God and He knows the happiness that I need. He was able to pull the rib from Adam to create a woman. Genesis 2:18: "Then the LORD God said, 'It is not good for the man to be alone. I will make a helper who is just right for him.'" I know I am a virtuous woman, and my soulmate will find me someday.

Marriage isn't easy. It should never be taken lightly. Stay with your own husband and wife, not somebody else's. You're getting the already-made products when the other spouse pruned him or her. Remember, commitment is two people coming together as one. Let's not get anything twisted. Get to know who your mate is by praying and asking the Holy Spirit to guide you and give you a discerning spirit. He will show you just who that person really is even before exchanging wedding vows.

There was no way I could have made it through without Jesus. His strength made me strong. He was continuously pulling me through. So many nights I cried, not understanding why these things had happened to me, but I thank God for Jesus that He was constantly guiding me through. I could have lost my mind had it not been for Jesus. There are many situations in life that do get too hard to bear, but I am here to tell you that Jesus can and will see you through. Without Him holding my hands, there was no way out for me, but God said in His Word that "when I am weak, then I am made strong" (2 Cor. 12:10). I tried so many times to figure it out, but all I know is it was Jesus. I felt Him moving in my heart, on my sick bed, in the court house, on the job, in the hospital room, and at the doctor's office, and still did not lose my mind.

We are Still Standing

I bless my daughter, Jamari, for always being there for me. She believed in me then and now. We laughed, cried, hurt, and prayed together. Look at us now; we are still standing. She's blessed, and she is one of the reasons I wrote this book. Growing up as a young girl to see her mother going through life as a good woman, a good mother, and a good friend, she learned that marriage is sacred. Marriage is more than spats and disagreements. Marriage and love are a beautiful union because they are from God. God is love. In the book of Mark, verse 10:9, God said, "What I join together let no man put asunder." Anyone participating in any marital breakup, your blood is on it. God will deal with you in due time and season. Take time to read Ecclesiastes 3:1-8: "There is a time and season for everything under the Heavens."

I know my mother is smiling at me today, happy that I was able to move on with my life.

I give God the praise and the glory. To everyone that has helped me throughout these years of tears and pain, I

THANK YOU. I'm grateful for the weekly prayer calls. But most of all I thank God for always being there for me. I know better days are coming and better days are on the way much sooner than later.

I no longer smile from the outside in, but I smile from the inside out. I hold no grudges and I love everyone, the good, the bad, and the ugly. I love my life. I thank God for my struggles; I made it. I'm grateful that I don't look like what I went through. My hurt was my ministry. My pains are my testimonies to bless others. So, go and be blessed. Live life to the fullest because better days are coming. Take time to read the book of Luke, verses 6:27-28, where it tells us to "love your enemies, do good to those who hate you, bless those who curse you, and pray for those who persecute you. Your reward will be great."

I wanted to retaliate so many times against the other woman, to hate and hurt her and do the unknown, but God said, "No Mona." My life is more valuable and worth more than to waste my time on nothing. Be careful of the time and energy that you allow someone to have or that you put into someone else. You allow them authority and power over you. The question you must ask yourself, "Is it worth it?"

Pray Until Something Happens

You may wonder, what is PUSH? Thanks to my loving Pastor, Dr. Karl Miller, I learned that PUSH means "Pray Until Something Happens." Keep God first no matter what is going on. Here are some key principles that helped me get through all those dark and lonely days. Find some quiet time just for yourself; find time to pray. Spend time with God and tell Him all about what you're going through. Read daily devotionals and read the Word of God as often as you can throughout the entire day until bedtime. Take scriptures and apply your name to them and begin speaking those things that you want to happen into your life. Find a small group to connect with because it is a great way of connecting and sharing your stories, hurts, struggles, and disappointments with others. Listen to sermons and gospel music while driving in the car, and stay off of social media; and focus on things that will help you remain positive. Most of all, fast and always pray without ceasing.

We all have a story to tell. We all have a journey that can show others just who God is. Tell your story to bless others. Your life belongs to God, so share your story to bless someone else. I did, and I have so much peace, forgiveness, love, and joy inside my heart that ONLY God could give me. This is why I give God all the Glory. Be blessed and enjoy life to the fullest, because you never know what road you will end up on or how God will be the one to get you back on the right road. Your life is your testimony to others.

Acknowledgments

Book Instructor/Teacher: LaSonia Roberts

Dress Attire: Jamari Mon'et Wright

Photographer: Ukari Roberts (ukariroberts@gmail.com)

Make up Artist: Kenisha Juanez Maddox @ American Beauty

Inspirational Groups: Pastor/Dr. Karl Miller and CLC Worldwide Family, Celebrate Recovery, Dare2 B Different Ministry, Family and Friends.

9 781662 817052